D1738998

HOW TO RATE YOUR DEVELOPMENT OFFICE

A Fund-Raising Primer
for the
Chief Executive

ROBERT J. BERENDT
and
J. RICHARD TAFT

The Taft Group
Rockville, Maryland

Printed in the United States of America

Library of Congress Cataloging in Publication Data

Berendt, Robert J.
  How to rate your development office.

  1. Fund raising.   I. Taft, J. Richard   II. Title.
HG177.B47 1984 658.1'5224   83-50709
ISBN 0-914756-54-0

TAFT - Profit Thinking for Nonprofit Organizations
12300 Twinbrook Parkway, Suite 520
Rockville, MD 20852

10 9 8 7 6 5 4 3

TABLE OF CONTENTS

Section III: Problem Solver: Good Answers to Common Questions About Development and Development Performance 75

Acknowledgments

Any book, regardless of its subject, is the product of inspirations that exceed the capacity of the authors. And this book is certainly no exception.

From our years of analyzing the development programs and potential of scores of institutions and organizations, we have come across a few programs and, specifically, development practitioners, who can truly be classified as "exemplary." These professionals deserve to be acknowledged for the quality of their efforts in general, and for their specific input in helping to formulate the concept of this book in particular. They are: James W. Lambert, Vice President for Development at the Children's Medical Center in Boston; J. Edward Easler, II, Resource Development Director/Southeast for the Boys Clubs of America; and J. Michael Mattsson, Executive Director of Development at the University of Utah. Arthur J. Frantzreb, an independent consultant noted in the profession, deserves thanks for his useful and generous input as well, particularly in the area of staff/executive/board relations, an area of expertise. And special thanks are due to Philip Gray, Vice President and Chief Development Officer of Bard College, for providing a thorough and objective appraisal—and welcome critical comments—of this book at the manuscript stage.

Our copy editors, Enid Hodes and Fiona MacDonald, must be commended for their adroit editorial work, turning into intelligent prose that which was not before. And above all, thanks are due to Taft Director of Publications, Susan Ezell Kalish, without whose prodding, pressure, and professional judgment this book would not have been possible.

—Robert J. Berendt
J. Richard Taft

This book is dedicated to the memory of our friend and colleague, Douglas G. Bonner, Jr. His intelligence, taste, and gentility graced us all.

DEVELOPMENT BEGINS AT THE TOP

It is no secret that there is enormous turnover among those who raise money for nonprofit organizations. It has occasionally been reported that the average tenure of a development director at America's nonprofit institutions runs anywhere from two to two-and-a-half years—barely enough time for a development program to get organized and begin to show even a glimmer of productivity.

Here and there one can find success stories with real longevity . . . development officers who have served successfully at institutions for five, ten, and even twenty years. But these occasional examples cannot obscure the enormous waste of effort and money so many nonprofits endure in trying to establish solid fund-raising programs. One major medical institution reported recently that it had engaged six different development officers in eight years. A college we know of had four different ones in just five years. The story goes on and on.

Development people come. Development people go. Often, there are recriminations and anger. Accusations of being impatient or uncooperative. It is a repetitive scenario. The new or ousted development officer blames the head of the institution and trustees for failing to understand the problems inherent in launching the development program or moving it to a higher level. The manager and trustees blame the development officer for ineffectiveness, failure to communicate, or even worse—laziness and lack of commitment.

Years ago, we wrote a well-received article entitled, "When Development Directors Fail." In that article we explained to this specialized breed of folks why they often could not motivate institutions to become involved in the fund-raising process. We tried to explain why much of the problem rested with them, the development officers, whose role it was to make their professional and volunteer leaders comprehend the steps inherent in a successful development process.

Now, on the other hand, we have come to understand that there is another basic issue that needs to be addressed. Despite the fact that development begins at the top, with chief executives and trustees, the people who run nonprofit organizations such as hospitals, colleges, welfare or cultural groups generally fail when it comes to evaluating their institutional development programs. Many administrators, in fact, know nothing about fund raising at all—a strange but widespread paradox.

Time and time again, leaders of major institutions, complaining about a perceived lack of progress in raising money, have said to us: "I can't tell whether or not we are really on the right track. I don't know how much we should be raising. I don't know if we are making progress. I don't know what to expect or what to look for." It is a lonely and repetitive refrain, and it usually comes just prior to the difficult decision of having to fire a development director and start over again . . . recruiting, rebuilding, hoping.

For this reason, we feel that it is essential that administrators, presidents, directors—whatever their title or organization they lead—be educated on exactly what development *is* and how it is supposed to function. It is impossible to measure successful development in its early stages solely on the basis of how much money is coming in, how many grants or gifts are being committed, or how many donors are giving. Development is a subtle, institution-wide process involving many factors, some of which can produce money early but most of which are calculated to produce major funds in the future. For you, the chief executive, to understand whether or not the investment you are making will ultimately pay off, you must understand what to look for and how to measure progress in terms other than money alone.

We have heard frustrated administrators—waiting, in their judgment, too long for the fund-raising process to swing into gear—say: "Well, one or two large gifts would change my mind and vindicate the entire program." Yet it is altogether possible for a development program to generate substantial gifts and, nevertheless, be totally on the wrong road. We have seen major funds raised—the cream skimmed—with nothing permanent put in place in terms of continued cultivation, records, systems, and other ingredients of long-term development success. Occasionally, we have seen all the essentials put in place and yet enough money never raised to satisfy the fantasies and hopes of the administrators of institutions.

This is a book about evaluating development performance. But it is also a book dedicated to the proposition that fund raising is a cooperative process requiring both understanding and communication going in two directions—from the administrators and trustees down to the professionals who administer development, and from the development people on up to those who need to know and have come to expect development results. It is our contention that if you, the administrator, know what to look for, understand your role, and can evaluate performance in systematic and professional ways, we will all take a large step toward eliminating destructive turnover in development and help to maximize the resources and investments of our institutions.

DEVELOPMENT: MYTH AND REALITY

After almost 20 years in the business of helping non-profit institutions to develop the systems, procedures, and techniques for finding philanthropic dollars, I can say honestly that I have seen very few top executive officers who understand fully how the business of fund raising and development actually works. This is not to say that I have not seen presidents of colleges, directors of hospitals, or heads of other nonprofits who were superb solicitors of gifts. I've seen many of these. Some of them seemed to have the Midas touch.

But even among the finest fund raisers I've known, I've rarely encountered an institutional leader who has had the patience, the time, or the experience to permit him or her to truly appreciate the dynamics of the professional development operation. There are exceptions, of course, such as the university president or CEO who has risen through the professional development ranks. In reality, such individuals are indeed rare—a telling commentary, we believe.

Indeed, this divergence of experience between the development officer and the nonprofit CEO is a major reason for the genesis of this book—a *different* book on the business of fund raising and development. Not just another book of conventional wisdom or fund-raising "war stories" for the experienced development officer. Not a compendium of tips or advice for the eager and aspiring fund raiser.

Rather, we felt that all the currently available literature had somehow missed the mark by failing to address the perceptions of the man or woman at the top of the institutional ladder—the chief executive. For it is the chief executive who vitally needs to understand exactly how development works. So we wrote this book, a book designed to help you:

- Understand precisely how a development office should be organized and how, on the most ideal basis, it should be run for optimum results.

- Measure the effectiveness of an established or new development operation in terms of goals ranging from money being raised to long-term potential donors being cultivated.

- Evaluate leadership qualities and effectiveness of the officer who heads the development department as well as the people who work in it.

- Establish a realistic salary scale for the development office.

- Appreciate your role as chief executive officer as it relates to development, so you can be more effective in fund raising.

- See the long-term importance of many things that come under the rubric of development, but often get buried under the day-to-day pressures of bringing in the buck.

- Value the guidance of board members and professional development staff.

- Understand the special roles of board members and professional development officers.

If we hope to achieve anything by publishing this book, it is to bridge the communications gap—and the understanding gap—between chief executives and development officers throughout the nation: a problem that produces turnover, waste, and inefficiency in thousands of America's leading institutions.

How many promising development operations get derailed because of this failure of understanding and communication? We believe the figures are mind boggling. For example, it has been reported that the average tenure of today's institutional development officer is about two to two-and-a-half years. The scenario is an old and weary one. The chief executive and board of an organization recruit a promising new development officer. He or she has a good track record. The chemistry seems right. Everything starts off with a glow of promise and high hopes for outstanding fund-raising success. A year or two later, recriminations are flying back and forth. The development officer feels that the chief executive is impatient and doesn't understand the process required to cultivate and secure gifts and grants, and has failed to take fund raising seriously. The chief executive feels that progress is inadequate, that the dollars are not rolling in fast enough, or that the promise of major gifts to come is unclear. Somewhere in the process, board members perhaps feel that they have been let down by both the development officer and the chief executive. On the other hand, the development officer feels the board has neither given nor "gotten" sufficient funds, failing to cooperate with the development staff. It is time for the "headhunter" once again. Continuity, morale, and progress all suffer, to say nothing of the balance sheet.

How can it be, in this day and age, when the financial fortunes of so many institutions rest upon the development program, that the heads of many institutions lack a real working knowledge of how development programs function? How can it be that so many college presidents; hospital administrators; or heads of welfare, arts, or environmental groups know so little about the basic elements of development— deferred giving, gift management and recording, annual giving, cultivation techniques, and so much more?

Can the heads of institutions simply turn *all* this over to a development professional, thereby washing their hands of the entire business? The answer, of course, is "no"; no more than the president of a firm which depends heavily on computer technology can abdicate responsibility for learning *something* about computers.

It is not enough to simply be available for an occasional solicitation. Today's nonprofit executive has a responsibility to understand enough to be able to *measure development performance* and make vital decisions about the future of that part of the institutional management team. That's what *this* book is all about.

Nonprofit institutions face a new era. Government largesse has greatly diminished. Corporate and foundation giving cannot fill the gap. Human needs are greater than ever, and the competition for funds is accelerating at a fearsome pace. At the same time, professional associations such as the National Society of Fund-Raising Executives (NSFRE), the Council for Advancement and Support of Education (CASE), and the National Association for Hospital Development (NAHD), among others, are helping prepare many more professionals for the development ranks. We believe, however, that all of this increased and badly needed professionalism will come to naught in helping America's institutions—unless the top executives comprehend, in some depth, how development actually works.

—J. Richard Taft

SECTION I: AN EXECUTIVE'S UPDATE ON THE FUND-RAISING BUSINESS

WHAT "DEVELOPMENT" MEANS FOR YOUR ORGANIZATION

"The old gray mare, she ain't what she used to be . . ." The old, tired fund raiser . . . he (or she) ain't what he used to be either. Before the 1940s, when one thought of the fund raiser it was with visions of:

— The blind man with dog and cup on the corner.

— The solicitor from a charity at your door.

— The charity "salesman" in the threadbare blue seersucker, ready to take his 40 percent cut.

— The campaign manager, arriving at your doorstep to harness the powerful board and raise great sums.

— The person who sent endless letters to potential donors.

— The head of the bake sale.

Many of these same images still linger in the "charity" field today. But along the way there has emerged within America's leading institutions a more sophisticated being, known as "the development director." In contrast to the 40 percenter, the "Casey-at-the-bat" campaign manager, or the blind man on the corner, this emerging full-time professional is often assisted by an army of well-trained professionals who understand computers, estate planning, marketing, design, corporate and foundation relations, psychology, research, publications, and many other aspects of fund raising as practiced today. And the best people in development scarcely resemble a "fund raiser" in the old sense. The best are far-sighted financial planners and strategists who know how to mobilize the full resources of an institution for maximum gift, grant, and bequest return over the long term—a real part of a management team.

In this book, we will attempt to give an overview of many kinds of development operations. In the process, we may debunk a few myths about the quality of management of some of the most sophisticated development efforts in the country. For those of our readers who may be overseeing one of the 20,000 to 30,000 major nonprofit institutions in America that can afford to utilize extensive development resources and advanced technology, we will point out how development directors can overwhelm management with sophisticated—but unproductive—terminology. We will suggest appropriate ways to evaluate development performance. For our readers in charge of the tens of thousands of smaller agencies and organizations, we will discuss lower-budget styles of professional development efforts.

This book is also intended for the nonprofit CEO who is thinking of making the leap from the one-man shop, the do-it-yourself approach, the part-time operation, the volunteer or underpaid assistant to a slightly more advanced form of raising funds. If you feel yourself to be teetering on the brink of moving into that complex and much misunderstood world known as development, we think this book is just as important to you as to the president of an Ivy League university employing 50 full-time development professionals.

It is important from the beginning, in discussing development as it is practiced today, that we differentiate between the various types of organizations and the different modes of fund raising that may be appropriate to each. For you must know where your organization stands within this world before you can determine how a good development program is distinguished from the not-so-good.

Development/Fund Raising: Different for Every Nonprofit Organization

Recently, the president of an environmental advocacy organization asked us to help him recruit a development officer for his agency. He had previously sought such a person without success. He believed, however, that if he could recruit the right person for this key development position, he would be able to move the organization forward in much the same manner as some other large agencies, or perhaps even highly successful colleges or hospitals.

Our first inclination was to launch a search among development professionals to locate the best person for the job. However, we quickly realized that a development professional who might be comfortable in an academic or other institutional setting might feel totally out of place in an environmental group. And so, instead of conducting a fast search, we concluded an agreement with the organization to work with it for a number of months to explore its problems and opportunities as well as to delineate clearly the kind of person who might be most appropriate to the development position.

Before long, we came to understand several things. First, we saw this was a "go-go" type agency where everybody—roughly 50 people—pitched in and where lines of authority and communication were rather unclear. Second, we rapidly came to understand that the board of directors, unlike the trustees of the typical nonprofit institution, was made up primarily of environmental professionals rather than corporate or philanthropic leaders. Any development director arriving on this scene, then, would find very little fund-raising leadership with which to work. Third, we realized that this organization had no alumni, grateful patients, nor other readily identifiable constituency of individual givers. Its efforts in fund raising would have had to center upon corporate support or foundation grants, and perhaps ultimately some type of direct-mail appeal. Thus, the new development officer would have to be more expert in grantsmanship and corporate presentations than in leadership development, individual cultivation, or deferred giving. Finally, we perceived the staff itself as young and highly program oriented, and we predicted the staff would relate best to someone with environmental experience who could develop a capability in development.

Ultimately, we recommended a development professional with some background in environmental affairs. This person had good writing skills and a working knowledge of foundation proposal writing and grantsmanship. He was enormously articulate and presentable, enabling him to travel and make many lead presentations to corporate funding officers. This development job, then, turned out to be less the university-type development management kind and more the grantsmanship and corporate funding sort of approach. He used his executive director well and delivered an enormous number of presentations to a wide range of institutions.

All of this is said to underscore a very real bit of confusion that confronts you—the top executive—when it comes to hiring a development officer. This is that the development function can be totally different from agency to agency, college to college, hospital to hospital, arts group to arts group—depending upon the program, focus, and institutional makeup of the organization. In order to help you categorize your organization, let us present here some division of nonprofits and seek to explain the kind of development that seems most appropriate to each.

Universities. There is no doubt that universities and colleges have, in general, the broadest type of developmental needs and require ever more effective development professionals to help them capitalize on opportunities. First, many universities and colleges have a national orientation and thus can effectively deal with national foundations and corporations, and even the federal government—although government affairs is usually separate at most universities. The typical university also runs an annual fund among alumni, will solicit its own board and wealthy alumni for special gifts as well as major campaign donations, will approach parents, and will cultivate a wide range of alumni and outside donors for deferred gifts. In the university environment, every form of fund raising is employed—prospect research, special gifts, proposals, direct mail, special events, corporate and foundation relations . . . you name it. Within the college and university ranks, opportunities differ. Community and state education institutions often have less potential with national foundations; perhaps more with regional corporations, wealthy businessmen, or alumni. "To each his own" must be the motto.

Hospitals. Community hospitals often have development staffs that guide the solicitation of local businesses, grateful patients and their relatives, board, physicians, and others. The best of these hold successful annual dinners, cultivate significant bequests, conduct annual mail campaigns, maintain auxiliary and gift shop operations, and otherwise handle development in a highly professional manner. Nationally oriented hospitals and medical centers carry out many other components of professional development. Obviously, these great health-related institutions have stronger potential for obtaining operational and research funding from national foundations and the federal government. Some have indeed proven it possible to obtain support from international funding sources. Many have even come to understand the power and technology of television and have enlisted film stars and other glamorous personalities for fund-raising endeavors. Yet another layer of professionalism is required for this type of outreach.

Cultural and Arts Institutions. Museums, theater companies, dance groups, and other arts entities also have the potential for successful development programs. By and large, most of these programs have a regional or local focus, since arts institutions—like local hospitals—tend to serve people in their own areas. Such organizations must build and motivate boards with sound leadership, cultivate local and regional corporations and foundations, solicit wealthy individuals, and even conduct annual campaigns focused upon subscribers and friends. Research, proposal writing, special campaigns, and other professional techniques comprise the development effort at such institutions and can be fairly sophisticated at the larger arts organizations. Obviously, some arts institutions, such as major national museums, symphonies, or theater organizations, can also reach beyond their own region to seek national corporate assistance, foundation aid, and even major individual gifts. Arts organizations have been moving rapidly to hire development professionals and build development departments, and we believe that any arts organization with a budget of $350,000 or more should consider hiring a professional in the development field.

Welfare and Social Service Organizations. In general, most of the agencies that fall into the welfare category operate at the local level, and often benefit from participating in local United Way campaigns. Such agencies are prohibited frequently during certain periods from seeking gifts and grants for general support from community funding sources, but are allowed to seek support for special projects or even a capital campaign. These kinds of agencies sometimes find it difficult to use the full capabilities of an advanced development professional. Rather, people with skills in grantsmanship, perhaps direct mail, and even special event promotion fit more neatly. Indeed, many of the people working for agencies of this type work with "grass-roots" fundraising methods rather than with the sophisticated methods of institutional development. Everything from auctions to bake sales are used to finance the thousands of agencies falling into this category. Many of these programs depend on the overhead of federal or local government grants to support their efforts, a dependency that frequently has serious financial implications.

Obviously, there are some agencies in the welfare or social service area which quite effectively employ sophisticated development programs. There are enormous national agencies that concentrate on programs of all types, just as there are sizeable local and regional agencies that can utilize the full potential of development professionalism. Indeed, Boys Clubs, YMCAs and YWCAs, and other groups can benefit substantially from more ambitious ways of thinking in development.

For welfare organizations, an additional issue to consider is the affinity of the "market universe" of users of the services provided and potential contributors. Colleges have emotionally attached alumni; hospitals have grateful patients. Museums and arts groups have appreciative memberships, but welfare organizations, special interest groups, and others may well have no easily identifiable constituency with close emotional or community ties. The appeals that must be made, then, are quite different from appeals of colleges or hospitals. A high degree of emotional appeal may suggest that direct mail is the right direction to take. And in other instances, quite frankly, an agency may be limited to foundation proposals or simply to fund-raising benefits. The important thing is to define, with considerable clarity, the scope of opportunity before blindly seeking the service of a development director.

Religious Organizations. Very few churches or synagogues, if any, have development directors. This is simply because the traditional methods of fund raising for places of worship have either been to pass the plate or to make a selective appeal to members of congregations when the time comes to build a new structure. When capital funds for building or construction are needed, a campaign director from a major campaign firm might be appropriate. This is not to say that some churches or synagogues could not employ development directors successfully. But the effort would necessarily be limited to special gifts from members, to family foundation solicitations, to special events or promotions, and possibly even bequests. National religious organizations use direct mail extensively and some special missions find it quite possible to approach foundations, wealthy individuals, and others for support. But, for the most part, most community-based religious organizations have done limited pioneering in the advanced techniques of the development field—and some may be suffering the results, as evidenced by philanthropic trends over the last decade.

National Voluntary Organizations. Finally, there are literally thousands of organizations in health, welfare, special-interest areas such as environmental protection, population, international relief, urban planning, medical research, and a myriad of others. All of these organizations have potential in development, whether that potential specifically includes direct mail, foundations, corporations, wealthy individuals, international funding, government grants, deferred gifts, benefits, or special events. The point is that every organization's program, appeal, marketplace, and potential is different.

In the end, the questions a nonprofit executive must ask before choosing a development path and investing in personnel are: "How broad is our marketplace?" "Can we deal with a wide universe of prospects and opportunities, or are we limited by our activities or other constraints?" The amount to invest in development, as well as the person to seek, emerges from the answers to these and similar questions.

So, as a chief executive, you must never assume that the hiring of a development officer or advancement professional is going to solve your problem. The person with a great fund-raising record at a hospital could prove a total disaster at a health agency that required direct mail and marketing skills. There is, of course, much "cross-over" potential in development. But you must learn how to match experience and skills with the marketplace. The typical "headhunter" or recruiter may not know enough about the fund-raising market and the problems involved in development to be of help here. And that is one reason turnover is so high. The bottom line in development recruitment is that CEOs themselves must ultimately rely upon their own understanding of the dynamics of their organizations—both internally and externally.

DEVELOPMENT: STATE OF THE ART

Just as marketing is the process employed by commercial companies to influence prospective customers to purchase their products, so is *development* the process by which the nonprofit institutions influence prospective contributors to support their needs through gifts or grants. The similarities between the two processes, although they aim to achieve different goals, are striking.

For example, marketing involves research aimed at identifying and then defining the potential customer, understanding customer needs, positioning the product to correspond with the customer's characteristics, providing advertising and public relations support to build awareness, training salesmen to sell, and numerous other tasks and techniques. In much the same vein, development involves understanding the donor marketplace through "prospect" research, defining an institutional position, creating giving opportunities, building awareness through communications, training board members to "sell" to donors, and much more.

Commercial organizations feel comfortable with the concept of marketing and sales because their foremost goal is profit. By contrast, nonprofits, which see their primary goals in social service, education, health or other terms, feel less comfortable with the commercial terminology of marketing. So, to add prestige to the business of fund raising, someone coined the term "development." Other terms, such as "institutional advancement" or "resource development," are occasionally substituted, but it is essentially all the same.

The Art Is Just Developing

The skills involved can be most complex and demanding, perhaps even more so than in commercial marketing. Superb interpersonal communications and writing skills, understanding of prospect research techniques, leadership qualities, salesmanship, understanding of psychology, knowledge of tax law, and many other disciplines contribute to the art of development. Just as commercial marketers have segmented audiences, development professionals must contend with the young and the old, with foundations, with corporations, with wealthy individuals. And these audiences all break down into subcategories as well, each with its own foibles and subtleties.

Strangely, only now is the art of development beginning to advance rather rapidly, after years of virtual stagnation. For until recently, development was not perceived as a vital art and received little of the respect accorded to commercial marketing. Indeed, while there long have been college courses and degrees in marketing, advertising, and related fields, there has been no special university-related body of knowledge nor degree programs in the development field. There have been seminars on fund raising, on direct mail, and, more recently, actual credit programs in development at some institutions. But recognition for this art has come slowly.

This phenomenon is not too hard to understand. Prior to the late 1960s and early 1970s, which might be called the "dawning of the age of competition" in the nonprofit field, many colleges, hospitals, and other groups maintained something of an elitist attitude about promoting themselves too actively. Many educators felt it was somewhat demeaning to think about "selling" their institution to donors, or to prospective students, for that matter. Museums felt that their fine collections and cultural efforts spoke for themselves, pursuing major funds primarily when building expansions were required. Hospitals, seen as a perpetual growth industry, only worried about fund raising if there was a major capital need or perhaps a new research effort. Thus, the pattern of most institutions—including the major ones—was to tackle fund raising in a sporadic way, with major gift-raising efforts being conducted occasionally with outside help. Annual giving, deferred giving, and other development techniques were often neglected.

As inflation intensified and as competition for everything from students to patients to cultural patrons began to heat up, the financial pressures inherent in this intensified competition awakened institutional leaders to reality. Not only did they see the need for well-managed, ongoing fund-development efforts; but they also realized that major campaigns from time to time required a base of donors who had been continuously cultivated, involved, and informed. The annual fund became a more attractive concept as management realized the desirability of having an ongoing mechanism for raising money. It was also acknowledged that internal staff with sound capabilities were needed.

Other pressures also led to the advancement of the art of development. Not the least was the pressure foundations put on nonprofit institutions to define, with greater clarity, their missions and goals. This, in our judgment, is one of the greatest contributions foundations have made to the philanthropic field. It was the growing professionalism of foundation officials—the emphasis they put on long-term planning, budgets, evaluations, and other management techniques—that brought about new thinking and planning at many grant-seeking institutions. Foundations were the first to plan seriously about how to spend their philanthropic dollars, and develop ways to divorce themselves from the emotionalism of giving.

The emerging interest in planning during the early seventies thus heightened the need for better, more precise development techniques. Suddenly, just as the marketing personnel at companies realized that they should relate intimately to early product development, development people charged with fund raising pushed hard to be part of the institutional planning process. Indeed, they argued loudly that development was an institution-wide process that began with program and financial planning and ended with the actual taking of those plans and financial needs to the "market." The person who, traditionally, had been perceived as the "fund raiser" and had been isolated from the management process began to take on the image of a more sophisticated marketer, and even learned the language of the commercial marketing business.

With these changes—and very instrumental in bringing them about—came a group of emerging associations to promote the *professional* concept of development. The National Association for Hospital Development (NAHD), a tiny group in the early seventies, now boasts over 1,000 members. The Council for the Advancement and Support of Education (CASE) now has its own professional body of university and college development officers who share expertise and ideas on a regular basis. Development people in social welfare, churches, and other areas either have established similar type groups or are thinking about them. One group that has done much to help with the growing professional awareness is the National Society of Fund Raising Executives (NSFRE), perhaps an anomaly because of its name. The society has many fine educational programs and conferences and recently has sought to advance the concept of accreditation in the field.

Perhaps NSFRE's name underscores one issue worth examining. Many thousands of small organizations in every area have yet to reach the level of development sophistication epitomized in the full-blown programs of leading universities, hospitals, and other large organizations. In fact, while some major institutions may have development departments made up of 25 to 150 people, the more typical development office is the one-person shop—a place where everything from direct-mail letter writing to foundation research is handled catch-as-catch-can. It is here that the state of the development art should and must advance most quickly if these smaller organizations are to first survive and then compete.

Thus, there is an increasing willingness among growing institutions to put some money into the development process and to find the right person to head the operation. Indeed, there is even an emerging willingness to provide the dollars to permit these persons to hire specialists in foundations, corporations, direct mail, computers, deferred giving, proposal writing, and other areas.

The demand for experienced and truly knowledgeable development directors far exceeds, in our opinion, the availability of such people. This is the reason that many institutional leaders find themselves grasping at straws—recruiting for the key development position anybody who appears to have the capabilities to do the job. Unfortunately, there are thousands of people in the field—like any other—who have learned the "lingo" and who portray themselves as being skillful, but who really cannot deliver. Recruiting a competent development officer is no easy task, since it is exceedingly difficult to find a person who knows marketing, who can write, who understands prospect research, who can lead and motivate, who can manage, and who has a grasp of tax law. As a result, we have an enormous turnover rate in the development field.

Where Is It All Going?

One place it's going is up and up . . . in salary. Where the fund raiser used to be lucky to be paid $15,000, salary estimates of $60,000-plus as of 1983 for development officers are not unusual. Another place it's going is toward greater specialization, as people gain expertise in one facet of development, such as corporate giving, or deferred gifts. In the future, the truly senior and experienced development officer will have come up through the ranks after serving in many specialized capacities. A third direction in the field is toward the commercial world. Many institutional leaders are beginning to understand more clearly the parallels between development and marketing, and are turning to commercial companies for businessmen who might bring their skills and experience to the nonprofit field. We know of at least three or four institutions that have had considerable success "stealing" corporate managers and putting them in charge of the institutional development program.

Of course, development is moving into the era of computerized information technology. Years ago, the development or fund-raising office kept donor records and general research information on three-by-five cards. Today, hardly a sophisticated organization can be found that hasn't plunged into the computer age with some fervor. And the systems for gift information retrieval and word processing are advancing the development business at a rapid pace.

Organizations are today utilizing everything from telemarketing to teleconferencing for fund-raising purposes. One international organization held a benefit beamed by satellite to 227 cities where members, friends, and donors viewed a special presentation. Everything from cable fund-raising promotions to charging contributions on credit cards is being tried, and the range of marketing opportunities for reaching donors will continue to grow with the advent of more advanced technologies. Small organizations, too, will enjoy these opportunities and gradually move up in management sophistication . . . the inexpensive microcomputer is already being used by thousands for everything from financial planning to list management.

Perhaps the most rapidly growing aspect of the development art is deferred giving. Many nonprofits are learning that a sound understanding of tax law and some long-term vision can lead to healthy endowment building through bequests and other tax vehicles. There are even programs for small computers now that can be used to compute instantly a charitable tax benefit right in front of a potential donor. And other products are certain to emerge.

Ultimately, it is possible that the art of development may advance so far that the entire process of securing funds—both charitable and noncharitable—will be put under the auspices of a single "institutional marketing" office. This office will be responsible for earned as well as philanthropic income, including gifts, grants, product or service sales, membership revenues, and the like.

Whether you're more comfortable calling it an art or a science, the business of philanthropic fund raising has come quite a distance over the last two decades. To be sure, changes in the economic climate of the times, changing social priorities, and new developments in technology have changed the face of this business. But attitudes—always the hardest ingredient to gauge with any accuracy—have changed, too, and continue to change. No longer is the fund raiser someone responsible only for carrying the proverbial hat. Today, and tomorrow, the best people are and will be development professionals who are part of a management team— people as essential to the prosperity of their institutions as their counterparts in finance or institutional planning.

YOUR ROLE IN DEVELOPMENT AS CHIEF EXECUTIVE

No matter how large or small a commercial company may be, responsibility for its success or failure in literally every area of activity can be traced back to the chief executive. And so it is in nonprofit organizations. If staff turnover is far too great, *you* may have chosen the wrong personnel director. If programs are not working or staff are going over budget, then somehow *you*, as the leader, may have failed to establish clear goals or adequate methods for control. If morale is low, *you* may not be giving the necessary support to staff. And so it goes.

Why, then, is it so common in so many institutions for chief executives or administrators to be involved in everything from personnel strategies to new pro-grams—but not in *development*? Somehow, the business of raising money gets shuffled into the specialty area and is left to the development officer. The only time senior management tends to get involved is when deficits are cropping up and everybody is wondering why the or-ganization isn't raising *more* money. We can show you

college or hospital presidents, heads of research insti-
tutes, urban development groups, and arts organizations who stay as far away from fund raising as they
possibly can.

That isn't the way it works. Fact is, if fund raising isn't
producing the results your institution needs, it may
actually be *your* fault. That's because you are a very
central figure in the development process. For any development department *to truly function at its optimum
level*, you have to understand your role. Don't just keep
hiring and firing development officers and blaming poor
results on them. Instead, examine your own knowledge
and attitude about fund raising and gain a grasp of your
appropriate involvement.

Planning

As the head of your organization, you should understand that a development operation cannot function—
let alone be productive—without a clear-cut sense of
mission and long- and short-term goals. Not only is it
impossible to make a good fund-raising case for an
institution without a long-term plan—it is also impossible for the development department to identify funding
strategies without a precise understanding of institution
priorities.

As CEO, then, it is your responsibility to stimulate and
lead the planning program and to help determine operational goals and financial priorities. What is more, it is
vital that you include the development department in
that planning process so that it can participate in and
provide its own version of marketing and funding
opportunities.

Too many institutional leaders fail to include development professionals in the strategic planning process. When goals are established and financial needs projected, only then is the strategy handed to the development department. That is like a commercial company that spends time and money on the development of new products without ever asking the marketing department whether or not anybody will want to buy these products. Top business leaders today know that the marketing person must be included in all aspects of corporate planning. You should make it *your* job to see that your development officer is also included in your institution-wide planning process. It will pay dividends.

Stimulating Cooperation Between the Board and the Development Staff

Many nonprofit leaders leave the business of development exclusively to a board committee and the development department. Frequently, when fund raising is slower than hoped for, board members end up blaming development people and development people end up blaming boards. It is the role of the chief executive officer to foster a strong sense of cooperation between the development office and the board. If you expect to create a synergistic team to help your organization with fund raising, you must put some effort into creating this team. This means providing every opportunity for your senior development officer to meet and work with board members on a peer level. It means constantly cultivating your own board and keeping them informed as to the goals and needs of the institution. And it means being sensitive to communication between board and development staff, encouraging this communication at every turn.

Fighting for the Right Investment

It's a rare board member who doesn't think the organization he or she stewards isn't spending too much on fund raising. It's amazing how the board member who gives nothing and contributes nothing can holler and scream when fund raising speaks up for an extra budget or allowance. As chief executive, it is your job to examine with care the financial needs of your development department and to fight for that department so that it doesn't have to operate on an underfinanced budget.

Too many chief executives cut the fund-raising budget as soon as operating revenues get a bit lean. Just as years ago, many financial executives who ran corporations slashed the advertising budget as soon as business conditions worsened. But many enlightened business leaders with backgrounds in marketing came to understand that if you don't invest money in marketing and advertising, you don't keep sales up. So it is with development. You can't prepare foundation proposals without a writer. You can't find the big prospect without prospect research.

It is your responsibility to understand that you can't pare operating expenditures to the bone and still harvest bountiful development dollars. Invest carefully in development—but invest.

You Are the Spokesman

You've probably heard it said that college presidents spend 50 percent of their time fund raising. That may seem like an inordinate amount of time, but it really isn't. Who else is better prepared to be the spokesperson for your institution to potential donors and friends than you—the chief executive? Frankly, most donors—be they corporations, foundations, or individuals—don't want to see the director of development. They want to see you or your board chairman—or someone they know who is close to the institution. It remains all too true that, in a large number of cases, *you* must be the person to present your cause. Your development director may assist you. Your board chairman may join you. But nobody speaks better for a nonprofit than the leader of that nonprofit. So, if you don't think of yourself as a fund raiser, think again—or at least recognize that it's time to learn.

Those are some of the basic roles in development that any nonprofit executive needs to understand. But don't forget that there are scores of other things you can do to help development along:

- Encourage your development staff. Stop by from time to time to chat, find out what's happening, and praise them for anything praisable. Remember that development is a demanding job with a lot of disappointments and frustrations. Morale-building is a very vital part of your job. Development people get said "no" to all day long, and they need a lot of counseling and encouragement.

- Make yourself readily available for public relations purposes, to make speeches to groups, for coffee klatches with potential donors, for cultivation events of all kinds. Don't have the development staff feeling as if it's an imposition to use your time in this manner. Money is the lifeblood of your institution and the institution will be in a healthier condition if you can keep this in mind.

- Keep your eyes open for donors and communicate your thoughts to the development staff. Too many top executives either keep their thoughts to themselves or fail completely to take note of fund-raising opportunities. Make fund raising a high priority.

- Keep your own top personal hit list, but make development aware of it. We've seen top executives work with development offices in ways that are brilliant: birthday cards to top prospects; roses to wives on anniversaries; special attention to patients whose philanthropy is sought; and so on. That is yet another stimulating role you can play.

On balance, keep in mind that fund raising is not some isolated function. It is the core of the effort to "market" your institution to givers, and you are at the apex of the project. Without your involvement, sensitivity, and leadership, development cannot work. So, if you don't expect to be deeply involved, don't bother to invest.

THE BOARD'S ROLE IN DEVELOPMENT

Throughout all nonprofit organizations there runs a common thread. It is that the stewardship of these organizations rests legally and morally with a group of people commonly known as the board of directors or trustees. Indeed, there are some 25 million volunteers in America. A significant portion of the time invested in voluntary activities is contributed by those people who see fit to serve on these boards.

Unfortunately, many of the executives who manage nonprofit institutions—be these colleges, hospitals, social agencies, or cultural groups—fail to understand the role of their board and may therefore be guilty of misusing what can be an enormously valuable component in the management and development process. In fact, many executives seem to use their boards merely as rubber-stamp operations, window dressing, or perhaps the source of a ready handout when money is needed. Failure to properly involve, cultivate, and utilize boards of directors is a major factor contributing to the failure of financial development at many organizations.

Obviously, board members have very difficult management responsibilities. Certain responsibilities are stipulated in the IRS tax code and certain state statutes governing tax-exempt organizations. Other responsibilities are the product of tradition. It is common knowledge that trustees should:

— Provide fiscal stewardship for the organization, make strategic decisions about investments, and generally guide the management and financial directions.

— Make inputs on specific management problems, supplementing the recommendations and thoughts of the chief executive and staff.

— Recruit other board members to positions of leadership.

— Lend expertise in areas ranging from the law to public relations.

— Give money, assuming that they have money to give.

— Provide professional information in specialized disciplines.

— Participate in fund-raising campaigns, benefits, and other special events.

Board members accept positions on the board of institutions for many different reasons. Some have a genuine interest in a particular field or charitable area. Some feel that it is a community responsibility to donate some portion of their time to serving on boards. Some have had a long and personal commitment to a college, hospital, or other agency. Some see it as a method of gaining social and business exposure. Some do it for ego gratification (not a few people serve on scores of boards with little involvement, if any).

Few board members ever join an institution because they enjoy fund raising and development. Indeed, among board members throughout the country, development and fund raising would, were a poll taken, probably rank as the most disliked responsibility in institutional stewardship. Show us a trustee of a nonprofit institution who really likes to go out and solicit money and we will show you a breed as rare as the American bald eagle.

It is possible, however, for you as chief executive to work with your board members in such a way that they will be an invaluable asset in the development process. And it is vital that you understand the problems inherent in using boards this way because they—the volunteer board members—should invariably be your fund-raising sales force, your outreach to individual, corporate, and foundation giving sources.

Getting Board Members Started Correctly

Trouble in the board/development relationship begins most often when new board members are recruited or chosen. Frequently, those who recruit—be they the executive director or other board members—are reluctant to talk candidly about the role a new board member will play in development. It is invariably better to be honest and direct with new potential board members and not to hedge on the fact that they will have to play a role in fund raising. Don't fall into the common trap of painting a picture of many tasks, but then adding: "You won't have to do any fund raising." Ultimately, that kind of statement will come back to haunt you.

Recently, we conducted a feasibility study for a national organization that had been planning, for almost two years, a substantial fund-raising campaign. The executive director was impressed with the depth and breadth of his leadership, which included many top corporate executives, wealthy people, and some noted political figures. When an actual precampaign study was conducted to determine the fund-raising potential of the organization, it was found that few, if any, of the board members had thought they would have to be involved in fund raising. Only a few recognized that they would have to make personal contributions. And, by and large, most of them felt that communication about the program plan and fund-raising needs had been so poor as to make a successful fund drive almost impossible.

No institution can be successful in development without a board that is trained and committed to fund raising. Therefore, it is vital that you—as chief executive officer—and your development staff conduct a continuing program to involve, cultivate, and educate your board members on development. This doesn't mean hitting them over the head with all your financial problems. It means getting them involved in substantive issues, the planning of long-term programs, the construction of a case statement for your institution along with review of financial needs, the review of prospect information and funding opportunities on a continuing basis, and retreats where techniques of solicitation can be reviewed and discussed. It means constant sharing of financial and programmatic detail between your office, the office of development, and your key board members.

Some board members excel at fund raising because they have substantial clout or financial leverage. Usually, those who give the most themselves are the most effective fund raisers because they have the "moral authority" and are in a position to talk with peers in a positive fashion. Such people are often put on special board development committees, and are involved on a regular basis with the development office. But you can't just bow out of this process. Care and feeding of such board members is something with which you must constantly concern yourself.

For example, one executive director we know is masterful at getting board members to go along with him on visits to corporations. Another chief executive rarely visits a foundation without being accompanied by both a trustee and his development director. Such team approaches can be orchestrated effectively for maximum impact and should be a regular part of your management process.

As chief executive, you play a major role in keeping regular communications going between the development staff and your board. Remember, no fund-raising campaign has ever succeeded by staff keeping the board isolated from the ongoing program and development process, and then throwing down a set of figures on the table when the campaign begins. The development process is a slow and methodical one that involves continuing cultivation and education of board members. Even a campaign may require a year or two of board planning, involvement, training, and perhaps recruitment if your leadership is not adequate for major gift work.

A board of directors must commit themselves financially each year if they are to be truly valuable in development. A board member who doesn't give has little moral authority or basis for asking anybody else. There is nothing mandatory about board giving in most organizations, despite efforts by some we know to set a minimum annual target for all board members. What is more vital is that you, as executive director, drill the board continually on the concept of "sacrificial" giving. This means that every board member will personally rank your organization as a philanthropic high priority and will give as much as he or she possibly can to both help financially and build credibility among staff and other donors.

The more you keep your responsibilities in mind in regard to development and your board, the more successful your organization will be in the fund-raising process.

SECTION II: THE MECHANICS OF A DEVELOPMENT PROGRAM: THINGS TO LOOK FOR, QUESTIONS TO ASK

RECRUITING THE RIGHT PERSON TO HEAD DEVELOPMENT

All over America the heads of nonprofit organizations are trying to hire professionals who can produce funds. Perhaps you are one of them. Or perhaps you run an institution that has for years maintained a development operation. If you are among the latter, then perhaps you are satisfied with the performance of your development staff. But it is also quite possible that you are quietly distressed or concerned that your institution doesn't appear to be living up to what you regard as its fund-raising potential. In either case, it is a fact of life that any development program is only going to be as good as the people you have running it and the support you give it. And that goes for the institution with the powerful, well-connected board or trustees and lots of generous giving prospects as well as for the organization with little in the way of power or outreach.

From the outset, one thing should be clear. If you are hiring, or have hired, a person with the idea that you were getting a "fund raiser," you are probably on the wrong track to begin with. Just recently, an organization serving the handicapped called us to ask if we knew where they might find someone who could go out, in their words, "to hit wealthy individuals, foundations, and corporations." They failed totally to understand that there are very few people who can serve as an intermediary, salesperson, or broker for an agency; that fund raising rests squarely upon the shoulders of the trustees and the executive director or president aided by a staff development professional.

Frankly, we tend to eschew the term "fund raiser" because we think there is really no such animal. Fund raising is simply the end result of a very sophisticated and complicated *process* that professionals have come to call *development*, an art not at all unlike marketing in major corporations. That is the most common terminology. Some call it "institutional advancement." Some call it "institution resources." But, in general—even though we have a national organization called the "National Society of Fund Raising Executives"—most people in the profession would prefer to be called development officers rather than fund raisers.

The reason for this quibble over titles is simple. The title "fund raiser" belies the job. The job in development is to create a process of outreach to donors through the careful organization and utilization of others within the organization seeking funds. *Fund raisers—hereafter in this book referred to as development officers—do not, by and large, raise money.* They do prospect research. They train volunteers. They write proposals. They prepare brochures. They set up record-keeping systems. They establish meetings with donors. All of which is part of the process of orchestrating the institution's management and leadership to participate in its visits to foundations, corporations, and individual donors. If you are wondering what your development department is doing. . .there's something vastly wrong.

But now, what about the person hired for the development position? What should he or she be like? What kind of personality should you look for? What kind of references should you check? What are the right questions to ask? What should you pay? What should you expect in return?

Personality Is Vital. Understand, from the beginning, that a development director may know all the buzz words and technology of fund raising, even be accredited through the new NSFRE testing program—or maybe the National Association for Hospital Development—but may nevertheless have limited capability. That is because, by and large, a principal prerequisite for a development director is to be a motivator—and being a motivator requires a certain amount of creativity, energy, dynamism, salesmanship, and aggressiveness. Motivational and sales abilities are not required just because your development director will be out there trying to get gifts and sell your institution to donors, but because your development director will have to lead and motivate your trustees, volunteers, program directors, and others if they are to become the salesmen for the organizations, as they should be. If your development director doesn't have both the enthusiasm and the capability to convey that enthusiasm to those who must be utilized in the fund-raising process, how can he or she be fully effective? It is also true that on many occasions, in front of corporations, foundations, or even individuals, your development officer will have to participate in the selling process along with principals of the organization. An inordinately quiet, dull, or inarticulate development officer is not going to be helpful in this process. It is no crime to be reserved or even inarticulate. Such people can make wonderful researchers, or perform all kinds of other valuable services. But development is not really the profession for them.

It has often been said that a good development director is also a good pest. This means that the person holding down that job must be secure, aggressive, and persistent enough to "bug" your trustees and other volunteers consistently without fear of rejection. Enthusiasm needs to bubble over. Naturally, development directors must have the skills of communication and be excellent listeners—for that is yet another way of involving and motivating people. But without the aggressive qualities to follow up, the most carefully developed strategies can fall apart.

To put it simply, when you are considering development directors, look for the salesmanship and marketing mentality. If the applicant couldn't sell you as the representative of some company, how can he or she possibly motivate people to become more involved with your institution? Consider—unfair though it may be—the appearance, dress, and general social background of the person you are choosing. Development directors must be able to create an almost peer relationship with board members and staff. If board members are largely an "Ivy League" conservative bunch, it doesn't make much sense to hire someone who will conflict basically with their images and value systems. Enough said.

Skepticism Is Okay. Some heads of institutions get upset or offended if the applicant for a development position doesn't immediately think that the nonprofit is the most dazzling and dynamic organization they've ever encountered. After all, many people who head nonprofits are socially and morally committed to the enterprise, and expect everyone else to see the virtues and importance of their cause. If you're one of these, you are making a mistake. You should consider it healthy if a potential development director grills you hard on why your institution is so important and what would happen anyway if it weren't around. Good development directors, while expected to be committed to the institution's goals, are trained to understand that the world is not necessarily going to beat a path to your door. They understand that you and the institution are competing with other organizations for the same dollar. They know that your own concepts of how the organization is perceived may not be in sync with those of the funding world out there. They know that many institutions duplicate others' services. They recognize that nonprofits are increasingly using the power of the mass media to tell their stories, and may be skeptical of how your institution has been presenting its case. They may have tough questions about the commitment of your board of trustees and your own willingness to get out there and slay the dragons in the fund-raising arena.

Thus, beware of the candidate who appears eager to agree with your assessment of the institution's importance. Be even more wary of the development director who tells you stories of great fund-raising success in the past and hints at similar great achievements for you. Be terribly skeptical of the development director who indicates that a program can be put in place quickly, or who says that you can expect early results from his or her efforts. This is rarely the case, and invariably there is disappointment and disillusionment as a result. Back away from the person, however articulate and bold, who implies that he or she can go out there and raise money for you. In short, the good candidate is the one who puts *you* on the griddle, asks tough questions, and promises nothing except exceptional effort and professional discipline and enthusiasm.

Checking Out the Candidate. "He was part of a major fund-raising campaign at his last institution. He is accredited by NSFRE. He is a member of the key associations. And everyone I talked to said he was capable. His resume was impressive, almost impeccable. So why is he failing?"

That kind of refrain is as common as the perennial complaint about high taxes. Why? Because it is very easy to be fooled about development professionalism, if you don't know what questions to ask and who to ask them of. It should be said from the start that many institutions don't check carefully on development people. Since development is rarely accorded the respect given to other management professions, there is a tendency to assign the reference check to lower-level people. Or, to grab at anybody who looks as though he or she has been with a good institution, especially if your institution is desperate to begin raising more funds. Hence, the "Peter Principle" operates as inexorably in the development business as in just about any job classification in the world.

Even many recruiters, supposedly skilled in the development field, know little about how to evaluate potential candidates. We've seen development directors move from institution to institution, ever upward in salary and prestige, only to be discovered ultimately at top institutions as lacking in most of the qualities that can make a program go.

To recruit successfully, there are certain basic rules that you must follow:

- Don't assume that the basic skills for development are there. Check out each candidate's specific abilities to write, organize, manage detail, and think and act quickly.

- Be sure about the personality characteristics of the candidate.

- Make sure other people in your institution— trustees, staff members, program directors, etc.— feel comfortable with the candidate.

- Talk not only to the former boss of the candidate, or to the head of the institution, but also to some of the key trustees with whom he or she worked formerly.

- Require that the candidate show you personally written material, and even test his or her ability to take a concept and prepare a proposal as part of an application exercise.

- Avoid people who have shifted jobs frequently in recent years, and have all kinds of reasons for doing so.

- Don't be overly impressed by association member-ships—they don't necessarily indicate ability.

- Find out as much as possible about the size of the staff and organization with which the candidate worked previously. Success as a one-man operation doesn't necessarily indicate the ability to manage a major development program.

- If the experience is there, don't be too concerned whether or not the candidate has been in your particular field before—health, education, the arts—because a good, motivated person can quickly and readily adapt to the specifics of a new cause.

- It's not a bad idea to ask an expert fund-raising consultant to chat extensively with the candidate to determine his or her true level of professionalism and creative thought.

What to Pay

Unfortunately, the prevailing sentiment in the de-velopment field is to pay as little as one can to the development director, since fund raising is too often viewed as an expense rather than an investment. The most common hope, especially among human services organizations during the fiscal austerity of the early eighties, was to find someone for $15,000 to $25,000 who could do the job. Universities and colleges, according to figures fielded around 1983, have been willing to move up to the $30s, $40s, $50s and considerably higher. Health institutions, long among the slowest to move into development, tend to pay even more.

Of course, many small institutions feel they simply cannot come up with the front money to pay an adequate salary to a development officer until such time as results begin to appear. Frequently, the outcome is that they pay little and get little. The yardstick for what should be invested is actually not just the size and the budget of the institution, but also what you as the administrator believe might be the potential. If there is every reason to believe that there is significant potential—perhaps millions of dollars out there among friends, foundations, trustees, corporations—then it is absolutely foolhardy to hem and haw over a few thousand dollars, if you think you have the right person for the job.

Long ago, some businessmen learned that it would be perfectly acceptable, indeed good business, if salesmen or marketing people made more than the principals in the company—if they could indeed produce the sales results. In the nonprofit field, of course, it is somewhat different. Principals in commercial companies own the stock, and thus are willing to pay large amounts in salary compensation to see sales and profits increase—and consequently their own equity expanded. But there is no equity in nonprofits. And there is the frequent problem of wanting to pay a development director $40,000, $50,000, or $60,000, but having to fight the internal political problem of that person's getting paid more than program people, researchers, or other staff members. Still, as those within an organization come to understand that they can benefit from a successful development program, it is a battle worth fighting if the opportunity to secure a superb development practitioner arises.

As a rule of thumb, here are some numbers that appeared to reflect the salary scales in the nonprofit business at the time this book was written.

Estimated Salary Schedules (1983)
Development Directors:

Organization	Type	Salary Range
Colleges and universities	Small liberal arts schools	$20,000 to $40,000
	Larger colleges and universities	$40,000 to $65,000
Hospitals and health insti-tutions	Smaller community hospitals	$20,000 to $30,000
	Larger hospitals	$30,000 to $50,000
	Major medical centers	$50,000 to $75,000
Cultural groups	Smaller community arts organizations	$12,000 to $20,000
	Large community and regional arts organizations	$20,000 to $35,000
	National arts organizations	$35,000 to $60,000
Human services, social, welfare, and religious agencies	Small organizations	$15,000 to $20,000
	Medium organizations	$20,000 to $35,000
	Major national organizations	$35,000 to $55,000

Within these guidelines, you should not hesitate to pay an extra $3,000 to $5,000 or even $10,000, if the *investment* appears to have the potential of a sound payoff.

Titles. Development officers can be very sensitive about the title you give them. Recently, we offended a very fine national development officer by referring inadvertently to him as a director of development rather than vice-president for development. And petty though titles can occasionally seem, there are some good reasons for examining what you call your development officer. Try to remember that this person must have a peer relationship with your trustees and the top people in your organization because he or she will need to work closely with them in orchestrating their fund-raising participation. It is difficult to achieve such a relationship without the appropriate title. Remember that your development officer is much like the marketing head of a corporation, and invariably these marketing people are vice-presidents because of the impact and importance of the marketing role.

If no one else in your organization has the vice-presidency title, then it matters little. But woe to the organization that offends the ego of a newly recruited development officer by calling that person director of development—or, even worse, director of fund raising. Other titles are, of course, cropping up. *Vice-president for institutional advancement* is one. *Director or vice-president of marketing and planning* is another. Choose your own, but make sure that whatever you do, the development officer is accorded the proper respect in the management hierarchy.

BUDGETING: LET THE MARKET AND YOUR GOALS DICTATE

We have proceeded to this point on the assumption that any good development and fund-raising program will depend heavily upon the caliber of the staff member that you have hired, or who is on board, to manage the program. Let's talk now for a minute about how you, as chief executive, determine what should be invested in either a new development operation or one which is ongoing but needs refinement, in your view.

There are all kinds of horror stories one can tell when it comes to budgeting for development. Not untypical is the small organization, with limited resources but a big appetite, that hires a development person and thinks that's the extent of the investment that will be needed. The lesson soon learned is that the staff member is just one part of the investment. Also required will be funds for travel (especially if the organization has a nationally based mission or constituency); monies for promotional literature; and resources for research materials, secretarial support, record-keeping systems, and other items. If yours is a small organization with a one-man shop—where that one staff member has to cover everything from corporations to deferred gifts, then perhaps you've invested $25,000 to $30,000 in a younger development person. Expect, then, to put at least another $25,000 into these other items. Indeed, there are those who would say that if you can't invest at least $50,000 in a start-up development operation, don't bother to invest at all.

True, $50,000 may seem like a lot to you, especially if your budget is under $1 million. And even more so if you figure that you won't get anything back on the investment for a year or more. But it's just not realistic to hire someone and not to give that person the budgetary support needed to do a credible job.

The larger your organization, of course, the more it can afford to invest in development. It's not unusual for very large national organizations, particularly universities, to spend $1 million or more on development, especially if the market potential for raising money is present. You will find at these institutions staffs of up to 50 or more people, covering each specialty in development—foundations, corporations, direct mail, special gifts, deferred gifts, proposal writing, research, records, benefits, and many other areas. You will find large institutions with substantial donor files investing significant sums in computers to track gifts, handle word processing, and generally manage the growth of the development office.

In the early stages of any development program, costs are always high as a percentage of funds raised. In fact it is often a "break even" proposition. . .especially when there is a heavy component of direct-mail fund raising at the outset. But, as a rule, once a fund-raising and development program is running smoothly and efficiently, a national organization will spend about 15 percent of the funds raised annually on the staffing and support involved in development. For example, an organization raising perhaps $1 million per year, will spend roughly $150,000 on the program. Such figures can be skewed, naturally, by large bequests in any given year or by some special gift or foundation grants. But looking across the field, it is a statistic that holds fairly well on the average.

That figure changes markedly, however, if your organization happens to enter what development professionals call the "campaign." A campaign is an intensive fund-raising effort accomplished in a concentrated time period, and built around great organization and promotion. Generally there is a large goal associated with the campaign, which is most often for capital needs. Such campaigns are particularly appropriate to colleges, hospitals, and community organizations that can concentrate their efforts on a specific group of major donors close to the institution. They are less appropriate to national agencies, whose universe of potential donors is generally more scattered and less committed. Also, national organizations generally need operating or program funds, for which campaigns are not totally appropriate. In any event, the efficient campaign will generally bring in funds at a cost of 4–6 percent of the monies raised. The moderately efficient ones will cost 6–10 percent. And the less efficient ones will go as high as 15 percent. Much depends, of course, on the readiness of an institution to actually mount a campaign and upon the magnitude of the "leadership gifts" for such a drive.

All of these figures are very general. And much hinges on your mission, your needs, your marketability, your donor universe, your salary scales in particular geographic regions. Keep in mind that the ultimate decision that you, as chief executive, make in regard to development investing really lies substantially in what you believe, based on some sophisticated research or counsel, your potential is—and on what you can actually afford to invest. There is no question that some institutions with powerful boards, wealthy friends or alumni, or other highly positive factors can command much more money and thus justify a far more substantial investment in fund raising. If your institution's program is unattractive to donors, if your board is weak, if your case is thin, or if there are other negative factors, why would you want to invest in development at all? You might be better off investing in revenue-producing activities to try to create earned income, or in some other method of resource development.

The point is, no matter what your development officer says he or she needs in the budget, don't make any major decisions without asking for a definite plan that gives you information such as:

— What is the fund-raising goal next year and over three years?

— Where will donations come from and in what amounts: foundations, corporations, individuals, bequests, etc.?

— On what basis are the projections being made: guesswork or some kind of pragmatic research and analysis?

— What is the case that will be made to the market segments?

You can't, of course, hold slavishly to this concept in every case. If you are just getting started and have no history of fund raising, it is almost impossible—even for the most expert consultant—to tell you exactly what your potential is. Some analysis might be done by comparing your institution to others, or through other means. But your initial investment is frequently risk money because it is so hard to assess the potential of a start-up operation. Consultants can do studies of established institutions and help to judge what might be raised in a campaign, or how much more might be raised annually under certain conditions. But even this is hardly what one can call scientific, and involves a good deal of gut feeling and intuition.

On the other hand, don't be misled. Too many development officers who are hired decide, without market data or real information on which to base investment decisions, that they will *build an empire*. Typical is the case we saw not long ago. A large health institution that had never had a development officer went head hunting and paid over $50,000 to get a person on his way up in another institution. Upon arriving, that development officer, without study or analysis, promptly hired a staff of six or eight people, including researchers, writers, an associate director, a corporation/ foundation specialist, and more. He literally demanded a budget of roughly $500,000. Before long, he and the institution realized that the potential appeal of the organization was going to be limited for a variety of reasons. Expectations were not met, and the development officer quickly lost credibility. Needless to say that development officer has moved on to another position.

The reverse is almost as bad. A small national agency recently hired a young woman to work in fund raising. The presumption was that she would immediately stimulate a growing program. This new professional promptly found that the agency had budgeted no extra funds for support, travel, materials, or anything else. She, too, is no longer there.

Much of this comes back to an issue that is at the crux of any development program's investment decision and ultimate success. Simply put, the issue is: What is the case, what are the goals, what are the financial needs, how strong is your potential market, and what investment can be afforded? Think about this key set of questions carefully before you proceed. Get consultative help if you need it to plan properly. In fact, demand it. Or else your budgeting and your fund raising may be off the mark.

STAFFING THE DEVELOPMENT OFFICE

One of the most common complaints we hear from the development officers in institutions is that their departments are too often "undermanned." They claim frequently that they don't have staff in adequate numbers—or with sufficient experience or skill—to manage the kind of fund-raising operation they feel their institution expects or deserves. On the other side of the coin, senior executives and administrators also complain frequently that they are paying too much in salaries and benefits to development personnel, and are not seeing enough in return. So, who's right in this debate?

Actually, both sides are. A one- or two-person development shop can only do so much. To expect that one person—or two—can successfully cultivate and secure corporate, foundation, and individual gifts, staff a board development committee, maintain a year-to-year annual giving program, and pursue special requests that you, as the senior executive, believe are important, may be asking too much. By the same token, the chief executive has every right to expect that a development operation ought to cover its personnel costs and overhead.

To determine the size of the development staff you realistically require, look first at two factors: the volume of contributed income you need to raise annually and the specific "market segments" of prospective contributors from which these monies are requested. As a benchmark, it's usually safe and fair to expect that a development operation should be capable of raising no less than five to six times what it spends for salaries, benefits, supplies, and other budgeted expenses. Mind you, this is not a scientific formula; rather, it is a basic "rule of thumb" that you can use to determine what you can reasonably expect for every additional development expenditure—most notably, for personnel.

More important, we believe, is what you might call "the penetration factor," i.e., the ability of your development office to actively—and successfully—pursue any and every reasonable giving opportunity among the full spectrum of sources, whether individual or organizational. If the staff of the development office is occupied to the limit of its available time, then certain other giving opportunities will invariably fall by the wayside. The best development operations are equipped to pursue any opportunity that is reasonable as well as carrying on such normal day-to-day or month-to-month activities as annual giving or wills and bequest programs. Assume for a moment that your development officer comes asking to add two or three new positions to the development office. What are some of the ways in which new people will be used? Rather than talk about specific jobs that a new person might fill, let's focus instead on the various development *functions* that can clearly occupy a full-time person:

Annual Giving. This term, as you probably know, is used to describe any program that annually solicits a body of contributors for unrestricted contributions. Normally such a program is conducted via mail, supplemented on occasion by telephone follow-up. Most programs begin in the fall, and involve three or more mailings in sequence through the end-of-the-year tax season, and often beyond. All in all, it's a time-consuming process that involves production of multiple letters, supplemental materials such as giving reports, segmentation of lists, etc. If you want the annual giving list to grow every year—as it should—then one person should be at the helm.

Corporate Giving. Particularly if your institution is located in a concentrated corporate community, you should consider making corporate giving a full-time function. The best corporate programs involve a large dose of corporate public relations—through letters, brochures, and the like—to keep the corporate audience informed of what you are doing. Corporate giving officers or other contacts should be visited. Internally, funding needs must be evaluated to "match" the right request with those sources whose giving history or policies suggest potential.

Foundation Giving. An effort to secure foundation grants should be a must in every development office. However, only in rare instances will it necessitate full-time staff coverage. Those situations that do warrant full-time institutional coverage are often in scientific institutions or other research-oriented organizations for whom *grant* (as opposed to gift) support is a necessary factor in maintaining programs. Frequently, the foundation giving function is divided: One person may handle government *and* foundation affairs; or, more commonly, will manage corporate *and* foundation affairs. The same kind of cultivation that is required for corporate giving should apply in the foundation arena as well.

Planned or Deferred Giving. This development function requires the largest expenditure of time and, consequently, expense, to achieve a return. Negotiating a will, bequest, life-income gift, annuity, or trust arrangement also requires a person with specialized training. In short, they'll cost you more, but the long-term returns (*not* short-term) could be substantial. A person responsible in this area will spend considerable time away from the office, much of it in lawyers' or accountants' offices, or in the offices or homes of prospective contributors. It's a process that can't be rushed.

Prospect Research. Large development offices often require a person to manage development records and conduct research of corporate, foundation, and individual prospects as a support function for staff who work in the field. The critical elements here are the people responsible for the actual donor contacts. If the background research they conduct is so extensive as to limit the time they can spend with prospective donors, board members, or contacts, then get someone to back them as a researcher.

Writing Services. Any high-caliber development office is going to generate lots of proposals and special presentations to donors of all types. Writing requirements can be quite different in each case. Creative writing may be needed for case statements or imaginative gift presentations. "Grantsmanship" writing, or what is called proposal writing, can require more of an interpretive writing ability, *and,* if an institution is technical in nature, scientific or technical writing skills may prove to be valuable. In general, the public relations staff cannot handle nor find the time for this kind of specialized writing. Some of it may be farmed out to specialists. But a high-energy development office will invariably need a good, solid writer to augment the efforts of the chief development officer.

Gifts and Records. If your development office is small or deals in a limited number of high-level solicitations, gift records and acknowledgment may be possible with one assistant or even a clerical person. But where you are anticipating a high volume of annual gifts, via direct mail or otherwise, someone to manage records systems and handle acknowledgments becomes essential. Indeed, many offices are beginning to have specialists in automation and computers to manage this function as the technology of gift information becomes increasingly sophisticated.

Just because professional staff may be added to the office to handle these functions doesn't mean that the chief development officer should be left to ruminate about matters of policy. The best development heads will be actively involved in every function of the office, as a participant, a source of guidance, and as the guardian of quality control. He or she alone is responsible for assuring that assignments are followed and the job is done.

Just remember, the next time your development officer comes asking for approval for a new position, that there are three questions that must be asked: 1) How much can be done with existing staff? 2) What are we missing by not having a person in this position? and 3) Do the opportunities in the marketplace justify this expenditure? If the answers to these questions meet with your satisfaction, then authorize the hiring of new people. Then you'll be in a position to see how the investment begins to pay off.

Section 2 / Chapter 8

SETTING GOALS AND PRIORITIES, AND HOW TO COMMUNICATE THEM

If your development director or department seems to be rowing hard every day, paddles flailing, lots of activity, paper flowing in all directions, meetings, solicitations, memos—but you still have the vague feeling the boat is going nowhere, you may be right. Activity in itself may have some virtue, but it can also be pretty fruitless without a specific set of goals and objectives, the attainment of which can be watched and measured over a period of time. Just saying that your organization wants to raise a lot of money through its development program will do little good. The money is the end. The development program is the means. But in between, there come a whole bunch of steps and concepts that you can understand and evaluate if you know what to look for.

First, and probably foremost, a development department has to establish itself as the conscience of the institution—the voice that asks:

55

— Where are we today and what are we selling to donors?

— Is what we are today what we want to be tomorrow?

— Do our potential giving publics perceive us in the same manner that we perceive ourselves?

— Do they, by and large, approve of our work and endorse our objectives for tomorrow?

— What kinds of financial resources will we need to finance the objectives we have in mind for tomorrow?

— What are our financial priorities in everything from construction to program funds?

— Are the people in our institution behind our vision and do they understand the goals ahead?

— With whom are we competing, and is there anything particularly unique or distinctive about our approach to the field?

— How do we best communicate our distinctions, goals, and objectives to our publics?

— Where do our trustees and volunteers fit in?

— How do roles of management, trustees, and staff complement each other in the development process?

It matters not how great, old, or distinguished your institution may be. If your development director and department have not asked these questions, and asked them recently, then you can assume that there is something wrong. Because any sensitive and effective development director understands that he or she operates in a competitive marketing climate, butting heads with literally thousands of institutions that claim to have vital and deserving goals. You are in a battle, whether you like it or not. It's you or them. And no development or marketing director who knows that selling means "positioning" your institution correctly in the marketplace will fail to engage you and your staff in this kind of dialogue.

In the commercial world, the concept of "positioning" has become perhaps the most critical word in marketing. It sets the stage for all communications, sales, and advertising programs. It means discarding your cloak of virtue, looking long and hard at what you really have to sell, examining competition and the openings in the marketplace, then driving your truck through an opening with all the communications power you can bring to bear.

In development, you will often hear the expression "case statement." Put most simply, the term, "case," is short for "case for support"—a statement of fact(s) about an institution used to argue for, or convince someone to make a contribution. The term has its origins in the legal concept of presenting a case for a defendant or plaintiff to a judge and/or a jury. All right, that seems basic enough. So where's the confusion? The confusion stems from whether or not a case is intangible (like a concept, philosophy, or theory) or tangible (like a printed booklet or brochure). The resultant discrepancy about what a case is and is not has tended, in our view, to obscure this important concept in institutional development and promotion.

Unfortunately, some development directors and fund-raising firms as well often think that writing a case statement is a simple exercise in putting down words that look good and seem to tell the story of the organization, along with its needs. The process is not often treated with the same care and marketing orientation afforded it in the profit world. As noted by Paul Schneiter in his book, *The 13 Most Common Fund-Raising Mistakes*, institutions waste millions of dollars on literature that evolves more from the ego than from the reality of the market.

On balance, then, one measure of the good development office is whether or not it forces you and your colleagues to think hard about these issues. If they are, chalk up one point on the effectiveness scale. You are at least on the first leg of the journey. Make sure that your development office takes some kind of measure of public opinion—friends, alumni, donors, corporations, others—before your program shifts into high gear. You want to be able to measure later how your program is affecting these kinds of attitudes, and, as in any scientific process, you need some kind of benchmark (or "control" group) to which you can refer. Too many institutions conduct attitudinal studies only when a big campaign is in the works. We need to take our temperatures more often than that.

Another very important role played by the case is the involvement of board members and volunteers in the planning process. That involvement will ultimately be vital to their willingness to get involved in actual fund raising. If you and your development department take the position that case development is a way not only of extolling the past but of also planning and envisioning the future, along with its financial needs, the very process of putting together that case can become the foundation on which your institutional fund-raising program is built. The process can be somewhat risky, of course. Everyone tends to think of him or herself as an editor and may want to get involved more in changes of style than substance. But in the long run, it will be to the institution's benefit if trustees and staff alike identify with the case development process.

When the case is nearing completion and becoming ready for design and printing, you should then ask yourself these questions, as the chief spokesman for your institution:

— Is the history and accomplishment of your institution adequately represented without being verbose or overburdening?

— Does the content and vision of the case inspire and motivate your board? Will they take it proudly to donors?

— Have you distinguished your organization, as much as possible, from your competitors?

— Does the case statement adequately justify and document your financial needs to contributors, or does it make too many assumptions as to their prior knowledge?

— Does the document identify with past contributors as a means of conveying credibility and value?

— Does the text convey various means through which an interested person can give to your institution—memorial opportunities like income gifts and other methods?

It is hard to apply absolutes to a highly subjective creative process such as preparing a case statement. However, there is one absolute criterion that you should apply to this presentation, without hesitation—if you're not happy with it, for whatever reason, it simply won't fly. You are, above all, the chief salesman of your institution. And if you're not happy with the principal sales tool, then it will be of little value. So, stick to your instincts and judgment about what's good and accurate and persuasive, and what's not.

If a case statement is being developed in conjunction with a major fund-raising campaign, then don't be miserly about its production. The appearance of the case statement should reflect the magnitude and importance of the needs it articulates, while not being unduly gaudy or extravagant. Once again, this is hard to dictate. But it is one instance where an investment in colorful and imaginative graphic design can pay dividends over the long term, through a document that impresses people. It's the job of your development officer to present you with a package that makes sense—creatively and economically. Remember, however, that taste is subjective, so speak out if the package doesn't work for you.

WHERE DEVELOPMENT ENDS AND PUBLIC RELATIONS BEGINS

A heated controversy has been going on for many years, not only pertaining to the role of public relations in development, but also arguing the issue of whether or not the public relations specialist at an institution should report to the development director. Indeed, if one draws an analogy between *marketing* and development (the latter being the marketing of the institution for all sources of income, including philanthropy), then public relations might rightfully report to development, much as PR relates to the marketing function in major corporations. In effect, the cultivation of donors is a form of public relations, although there are many distinctions that might prevent the analogy from being totally adequate.

In most circumstances where nonprofits have public relations staff, that staff generally operates independently of development, focusing on a variety of public relations goals designed to enhance the visibility and public image of the institution. This is standard in many colleges, hospitals, social agencies, and other large non-profits. And, for the sake of consistency, we have not listed public relations as a specific task or position within the development office.

However, as chief executive, you should understand that public relations must work closely with development and provide a fair measure of support if the development is to be successful as an institutional process. For development to be successful, individuals, donors, corporations, and foundations must have a positive view of your organization's mission and goals. Public relations also sets the tone for morale within an organization, morale which is vital to cooperation and enthusiastic participation of all employees and volunteers in the development program. Indeed, if there is a significant distinction between public relations and donor cultivation it is that in development there is one final step—the crucial one—*asking for the gift.*

Let's generally review the role of public relations as it relates to development, so that you can play a positive and proactive role in effecting cooperation between your public relations department and your development department.

First, public relations must understand fully the mission, financial goals, and case statement of your organization, so that it can establish public relations goals and targets that help your development office. If your development office places a heavy emphasis on corporations, your public relations department might be placing a heavy emphasis on securing visibility in major business publications, such as *Forbes, Fortune, Business Week,* and other magazines. If the chief targets are alumni, former patients, or other individuals, then the public relations department's ability to turn out high-quality print material keeping constituencies informed may have a tremendous impact on your institution's ability to raise funds.

Second, your public relations department may have a vital role to play in organizing and publicizing special events. Special events play a significant role both in cultivating donors and securing direct funds (i.e., the $100-per-plate dinner). Public relations must work closely with development to coordinate support for such activities.

Public relations must communicate a positive image not only to key donor markets, but to the general public as well, so that development has an opportunity to win *new* friends and to build its base of potential contributors. Where it is called upon for support in preparing audiovisual or print materials, it must work closely with development to create presentations that can have a strong impact on the donor market.

Some development people feel that public relations typically operates in a vacuum, never taking the time to put the program in sync with fund-raising goals. You, as the head of your organization, need to effect the kind of close cooperation that will assure maximum impact for fund-raising purposes. Listen to your development executive on this matter as well as to your chief public relations officer. There are real concerns with which you must deal. Timing, strategy, professionalism, and cooperation are essential elements in coordinating fund-raising and public relations efforts. In the end, a more productive development program—and enhanced visibility for your organization—will be the result.

SHORT-TERM AND LONG-TERM DEVELOPMENT: HOW TO ESTABLISH GOALS AND TIMING

If you have been looking at your development program with an eye toward understanding what it should be producing, both on a short- and long-term basis, you are probably susceptible to the same kind of confusion that besets other chief executives. Development directors often say, and rightly so, that the cultivation and closure of donations present time problems that can't be dictated and, thus, short- and long-term predictions are hard to make.

For example, many executives hope that a newly established development program will be able to produce short-term gifts from foundations, from corporations, and from individuals. Often, the chief executive appears to believe that all that is required is to ask, and the gifts will be forthcoming. In fact, institutional and individual donors take time—frequently lots of it—to cultivate and involve. Remember that the typical donor is probably less familiar with your institution and needs than you—who are closer to the situation—tend to believe. The typical foundation can take nine months to a year to review a proposal, make a decision, and forward a check. And individuals are often slow to be brought around to making a gift. Things normally improve at year end.

If you are new in the business, expect to see at least a year or so pass before you begin to see a trickle of short-term results. *You may be justified in asking your new development director for a second-year goal, but not for a first-year goal.* If something does come in the first year, especially something big, it is probably just luck. But what about the second year? How do you assess achievement? Well, aside from the bottom line, which will probably be modest even in the second year, consider these issues.

- Has your department a clear mission statement and set of financial goals?

- Have you and your board, working with the development office, seen a sizeable number of potential donors personally? There is an unspoken formula in development that goes something like this: "The money you raise is directly proportionate to the number of good prospects you have properly cultivated and solicited." Quality is vital. But volume is also significant.

- Has your development office developed and rated a significant prospect list—one that makes sense in terms of possible interest?

- Are the letters and proposals being written of high quality?

- Does the public relations program seem to be in step with development goals?

- Are your staff and board enthusiastically involved in the development mission? They can be able sales-men, and it is a role of development to cultivate their interest and help.

- Are prospect and correspondence files being de-veloped and kept current?

- Does your development department seem to have a plan, not only for the short term, but also for the long term?

These are some of the issues. Equally important is the longer-term issue of five-year development goals. Your development officer should be able to give you a strategy that says specifically, over five years, what levels of gift or grant income are hoped for and what is being done to attain them. He or she should be able to chart an antici-pated growth path in literally every area—alumni, grate-ful patients, friends, foundations, corporations, annual fund, benefits, direct mail, bequests, or any other area that is a part of the overall development plan.

And you should be asking tough questions all along about the gradual progress being made toward these goals. If, for example, your development officer tells you that more board leadership is required, then you should be asking about potential new board members and what is being done to recruit them. Only you can apply the pressure of reality with tough, pointed questions.

It would probably be wise to verify plans for both

short- and long-term results through use of an outside consultant or firm. A professional consulting organization can generally study market potential and give you a fair reading of what is and is not possible. Especially in regard to short-term campaigns, surveys can be effective if there is an identifiable body of potential donors who know your institution and who can be polled as to what they might or might not do in a campaign for a specific short-term goal.

On a longer-term basis, it may be possible for a consultant to provide useful evaluation of the size and strength of the potential market, and what a logical return might be over a period of one year. This is done partially through research, through some surveying, through comparative analysis with other institutions, through an understanding of a community or market, and, of course, through the experience and intuition of the individual consultant.

All along, remember that as CEO you are the true focal point of development, both as a representative of your institution and as the key manager. Development is an institution-wide process. But without your paying close attention to the program there is much potential for failure. Don't let your expectations fall out of step with reality. Patience—and hard work—*will* pay off.

RESULTS: EVALUATING YOUR RETURN ON INVESTMENT IN ORGANIZATIONAL FUND RAISING

This chapter is about results—how to determine what is possible and reasonable.

Ever since nonprofit organizations began raising money in a systematic manner, executives have wondered what results they should reasonably anticipate in return for their investment of resources. Since no "institutional standard" exists for what constitutes a fair "return on investment," executives of these organizations have resorted to various tests of the effectiveness of their development operations. Some simply measure the flow of dollars, and almost arbitrarily accept any amount over and above fund-raising expenses as adequate. Others choose to establish "time benchmarks," where the net income is expected to multiply by a certain amount over a certain period. Still others look for incoming five-, six-, and even seven-figure gifts as evidence that the fund-raising effort is producing at adequate levels. However, no single method of evaluating results works to everyone's satisfaction.

To be sure, this is one of the great enigmas and frustrations in the fund-raising business. By nature, fund raising is an endeavor of countless variables—any of which can spell the difference between a "productive" development program and one that fails to cover its own budget. In truth, there is no single standard—quantitative or otherwise—that can be applied to determine whether or not enough dollars are being raised, and quickly enough. Does this mean, then, that the relationship between you and your development professional is simply an "act of faith?" That the CEO can do nothing more than merely hope that monies come in? Of course this isn't so. But since fund raising is an often unpredictable business, the nonprofit CEO must be prepared to be flexible in evaluating the results of the development operation from year to year.

It is a fact of life that development is a long-term enterprise where results can neither be anticipated nor evaluated quickly. Certain kinds of contributions may require years of cultivation before an actual cash commitment is made. A proposal may be submitted to a foundation and then resubmitted a year later before it is approved. The factors that determine whether or not a gift or grant arrives in any given year are neither predictable nor controllable. As a consequence, to use the actual sum of contributions netted as the *sole* benchmark for evaluating development productivity is neither realistic nor valid.

This is not to say that, as the chief executive, you should pay no attention to the amount of dollars received in any given year. Quite the contrary. Rather, your evaluation should be based not on the amount of dollars, but on how the magnitude of giving compares with that of previous years and the time, effort, and expense required to raise the funds. Here are some rule-of-thumb suggestions for evaluating development performance.

Comparison with Past Years. Consider the comparison with previous years' giving. To be sure, a wealth of factors can influence private giving in any given year, to any given institution. An annual fund program that seeks unrestricted annual contributions—that normally come in relatively small increments—can fluctuate from one year to the next. Problems in the local economy, competition from another institution on a major building campaign, or even problems with a mailing list can all produce a drop-off in returns from annual giving. More often than not, the decline is temporary. If it's not, there's probably something amiss in the design and management of the program.

Growth in Donor Universe. In annual giving, direct mail fund raising, and other forms of "direct response" fund raising, *growth* is the key factor that you should look for as a measure of productivity. While certainly the flow of revenue is important, of equal importance is building a constituency of contributors—contributors who are dedicated and can be counted on for contributions in the years ahead. Naturally, there is nothing to guarantee that all your annual contributors will continue from year to year. The best annual giving programs normally lose relatively few contributors, but these losses are frequently more than offset by new contributors acquired. Another of the axioms in fund raising states that there is long-term value in getting people into the habit of giving to your institution, even if their annual contributions are small. If people are accustomed to contributing, they often will not hesitate to "stretch" their giving on occasion and give your institution something more substantial—say for a capital fund-raising campaign.

Penetration of New Markets. Fund raising is a dynamic enterprise that thrives on uncovering new sources of revenue and on developing new and imaginative strategies for securing that revenue. Therefore, you, as CEO, should reasonably expect that your development operation test—and eventually penetrate—new markets of contributors. In direct mail, this means testing new lists of individuals in hope of converting some to become committed contributors. In a corporate giving program, this may mean seeking out an introductory meeting with a representative from an area company that may be unfamiliar with your organization. Perhaps it means attending a service club luncheon to meet business leaders or to seize an opportunity to share your organization's activities with a captive audience. In short, the best development programs don't merely return to former or traditional contributors every year.

Quality of Effort on Foundation Proposals. Some forms of fund raising, particularly in the private foundation and corporate arena, are particularly difficult to judge in terms of results. For instance, a single proposal to a private foundation may be competing with 150 others at a meeting of a foundation's board of directors. The foundation probably has established a dollar ceiling for its grants committed during the period. Once the ceiling is reached, all other requests may be deferred until the next meeting—which may be six months away or more. If you, your board, your development officer, or others on your staff are fortunate enough to have an inside line, a contact capable of exercising influence, or if you are simply lucky—a grant may come through and in a timely fashion. But it just as easily might not. If the request is denied, does this mean your development officer is not performing adequately? No, because what counts in this instance is *effort*. You should make certain that the best possible effort was made by development staff to secure foundation support, including doing anything you can to influence positively the review of your organization's proposal.

Development Director Gets into the Field. Like the good salesman, the professional development officer must occasionally get out and "cover the territory." We have yet to see a successful development director who sits 40 hours a week, week in and week out, behind a desk. The best people in development see the necessity of getting out of the office—to visit with prospective contributors, to call on a new company that may be a giving prospect, or to take a valued trustee to lunch. This kind of quality, face-to-face contact is essential to productive fund raising. So be concerned if your development officer is spending too much time *in* the office, not out of it.

If at all possible, try to avoid comparing the results of your development program with that of another institution. However comparable they may be in size, no two institutions are enough alike to justify a valid fund-raising comparison. The variables of financial needs, board strength and involvement, and past fund-raising experience can make institutions that appear similar on the surface very different in the final analysis.

The return on investment from an institutional development program simply cannot be measured with a traditional quantitative or chronological yardstick. Like any other investment, an investment in development entails an element of risk. There is never a guarantee that the monies invested will be multiplied. Years may pass before a desired gift or bequest comes to fruition. Just as easily, years may be spent in cultivation, only to have the eventual gift from a donor fall far below expectations. In short, in dollar terms, it will always be problematic to classify what constitutes a "good" return on investment. In terms of effort and professionalism, you're on solid ground in expecting a great deal. For without that effort, the investment simply won't measure up.

PROBLEM SOLVER: GOOD ANSWERS TO COMMON QUESTIONS ABOUT DEVELOPMENT AND DEVELOPMENT PERFORMANCE

Throughout this book, we've emphasized the fact that no two fund-raising programs are ever completely alike. Programs at similar organizations may share certain characteristics but, in the end, the human factor in this "people business" of fund raising makes every organization's situation special—and maybe unique—in one way or another.

Because there are similarities, however, we've learned that chief executives frequently have similar problems in understanding development, and frequently pose similar questions. Here are some of the more common questions that have been posed to us and to others. More important, we've attempted to match a viable answer with each question. While neither the question nor the answer may be directly relevant to your organization, maybe you'll find a clue that will be.

☑ **Q. There are few things I dislike more than asking for money. What role should I play in development?**

A.   Regardless of what anyone might say about the virtues of philanthropic fund raising, certain people retain a strong dislike of asking for money. Others feel that, because of their personality, their manner, their general way with people, or some other characteristic or idiocracy, they are somehow ill-equipped to participate in fund raising. The fact is that certain people do better at fund raising than do others. But, because you might not enjoy fund raising is no excuse to avoid it. If you really do dislike fund raising, then we'd say that you should reserve yourself for those situations where your presence as chief executive can truly make a difference. In other words, use yourself sparingly, but don't think that you can abdicate your responsibility to represent your organization in fund-raising situations. There are certain to be situations where your presence *can* have a positive impact, whether you actually enjoy yourself or not. So our advice is "learn to live with it." You may be one of those people for whom fund raising is a necessary evil. Find a way to make yourself comfortable with the role of spokesman. And remember, people often expect to be asked for a contribution from someone in your position at one time or another.

☑ Q. **How do I—as chief executive—determine whether or not I'm spending enough time in fund raising?**

A.   As with many things related to fund raising, the combined judgment of you and your development officer will be the best guide. As a rule, however, the demand on your time will normally vary with the kind of fund raising that your organization is engaged in. For example, if almost all of your contributions are raised by direct mail, the demands on your time will be very slight. By contrast, if you're seeking a number of large, individual gifts from wealthy friends or patrons, your active participation could be critical—and this might be very demanding on your schedule. A critical part of any development director's job is using you and your time without *abusing* your time. Certainly, if other responsibilities are falling by the wayside because of heavy commitments to fund raising, you're probably spending too much time. Spend as much time as you and your development officer feel is essential—not simply desirable—to make the best impact and achieve the best results in individual fund-raising situations.

☑ **Q.** **To what degree can our problems in fund raising be blamed on our board's failure to take initiative?**

A. There are two critical considerations here. First, fault can never be assigned completely to the board, nor, for that matter, to the development officer. If you need active board participation, as most organizations do, then it's up to you and the development officer to provide leadership and guidance. If your board refuses to help and your program begins to slide as a result, then consider looking outside the board for voluntary help. Or in your next visit with the chairman, think about suggesting that new members be added to your board.

Second, don't let your expectations of board participation in fund raising fall out of line with reality. You are the person charged with managing the organization, not the board. Don't expect them to take much in the way of initiative; that's not their responsibility, but yours. Typically, the best boards of directors are willing to discuss strategy, but would prefer to leave technique to the professionals. And, more often than not, they prefer to be asked to do something specific related to fund raising.

☑ **Q. What can my development director do if our board lacks clout and giving power?**

  A. Many people make the mistake of thinking that only someone who has made a six-figure gift can effectively engage in fund raising on an organization's behalf. To be sure, it's important that volunteers in fund raising—including board members—make a financial commitment themselves before asking others to do the same. The size of the commitment is actually less important than the commitment itself. So even a board comprising the less-than-wealthy can be well-motivated, and do quite well in fund raising.

Clout is relative to the kind of organization you manage, where you're located, and the scope of your dollar needs. Clout means influence. If you're located in a big city, and are a prestigious institution seeking millions, then a large measure of influence will be needed to extract the large commitments you'll probably feel are required. For a smaller organization, the needs will be more modest. In other words, not every organization needs the local bank president, company CEO, or prominent socialite on the board to be successful in fund raising. Chances are you have more "clout" available to you than you may realize.

☑ **Q. When will we be ready to seriously consider launching a fund-raising campaign?**

A. By definition, fund-raising campaigns are characterized by pressure, an unusually high pitch of intensity, lots of promotional push, and strict deadlines. This combination, proper organization, and, as some say, the proper "chemistry," can make a campaign succeed in amazing ways. They can also make it fail, and fail miserably, much to an organization's embarassment. The first thing to consider in deciding whether or not to risk such a venture is financial need. Usually campaigns are run to support big and uncommon financial needs—construction, renovation, endowment, or other needs not necessarily related to day-to-day operations. Many organizations elect to have an outside firm conduct a "feasibility study" to determine if the campaign is feasible—if the dollars can be raised from certain identifiable constituencies. On balance, the financial considerations that will dictate whether or not you're really prepared to assume the risk of a campaign are evidence of gradual growth in year-to-year giving; growth in the number of contributors; consistent giving from the board of trustees; and the presence of valid giving prospects for significant "leadership gifts" that can be used to stimulate others. If all of these factors are in place, and the magnitude and the validity of your financial needs can appeal to contributors, then perhaps the time has come to put a campaign into gear.

☑ **Q. We're located in a city with a good number of institutions. How significant a factor will competition be in our fund raising?**

A. In virtually every community, there is bound to be some overlap among the contributors to various institutions. Studies have shown, however, that it is common for people to contribute voluntarily to more than one organization and agency. So among individuals, competition may have only a negligible impact, and certainly the failure of a fund-raising program to prosper can't be blamed on competition from other organizations. In corporate and foundation giving, however, the situation is somewhat different. These sources allocate a certain dollar amount to give away every year, and rarely exceed that budget level. A company may choose to spread its community contributions around among a number of worthy organizations, or it may restrict its giving to a few. So in this arena, it's possible for another organization to step in and secure a contribution that, under different circumstances, you might have received.

☑ **Q. What do we need to raise an endowment?**

A. *Everyone* would love to have an endowment, and for obvious reasons. Receiving a lump sum of capital that will both grow and provide income is naturally very desirable. It is also among the most difficult to obtain. Experience suggests that those organizations capable of developing endowments are those that have long-standing relationships with their contributors—such as a college may have with its alumni. This is because wills and bequests are the principal means by which endowments are built. On occasion, people will make endowment contributions. On rare occasions, foundations will also contribute. But unless you have identifiable sources who are truly committed to your organization, and have been so for a long time, it may not be worthwhile seeking this kind of giving vehicle. Don't expect your average year-in-year-out contributor to make an endowment contribution. It requires a different approach and a significantly different caliber of contributor.

☑ **Q. How long can I expect my development officer to stay in the job?**

A. Through an informal study conducted recently, it was determined that the average tenure of a development officer was between two and two-and-a-half years. By anyone's standards, that's alarmingly short. But, of course, it's just an average, and it's impossible to say precisely what you can expect. Just remember that the principal cause for the rapid turnover, in our view, is a lack of understanding between the CEO, the board, and the development officer. Like most things, understanding works two ways. If your development officer makes the effort—as he or she certainly should—to understand your requirements, demands, and priorities, you should reciprocate. Add the board to this mix and you just might defy the averages.

☑ **Q. When it comes to salaries in development, how much is too much?**

A. The first consideration is the existing range of salaries for other management positions in your organization. Naturally, you don't want the development director's salary to be too much out of line with those of other positions of equivalent responsibility. The salary you pay should be commensurate with the scope, complexity, and demands of the fund-raising program. The higher the pressure and demands, the more you need an accomplished professional—who, consequently, will cost more to retain. The price you pay is too much if the operation doesn't produce and doesn't grow in numbers of givers and amount per gift.

☑ **Q. How can I help to facilitate better understanding between the development officer and other senior staff?**

A. In far too many organizations, development doesn't get the respect it deserves as a vital institutional process. The head person in development is as much, and as important, a member of your management team as other senior managers. If you're facing a problem of poor communication between senior staff and development, that's really *their* problem to solve. You can help, however, in ensuring that development is taken seriously, by *your* participation in fund raising. You can be sure that as the results come in, people will stand up and take notice.

Section 4

GLOSSARY OF BASIC DEVELOPMENT TERMS

Advance gift—Contribution made in first phase of major campaign.

Annual fund—Yearly fund-raising program to produce operating monies.

Bequest—Gift made through a will.

Campaign—A special, planned and publicized, time-limited fund-raising effort.

Case statement—Document describing institutional history, goals, and financial needs.

Charitable remainder annuity trust—Planned giving instrument transferring certain types of assets (cash, securities, or real estate) to a charitable institution, while the donor or beneficiary retains a fixed dollar amount of annual income from the trust for life. Assets designated to the institution on death of donor or beneficiary.

Charitable remainder unitrust—Similar to the charitable remainder annuity trust, except pays donor or beneficiary a fixed percentage of the value of the trust's assets.

Clean-up—Last phase of major fund-raising campaign.

Cultivation—Efforts made to involve and interest donors over time.

Deferred gift—Gift which does not bring cash immediately to an institution.

Development director—Person who manages fund-raising office.

Direct giving—Contributions from corporations not made through their foundations, normally approved by designated committees of corporate executives.

Direct mail—Mass mailings soliciting gifts.

Endowment—Special and separate fund producing interest income for institution.

Feasibility study—Survey to determine fund-raising opportunities and goals.

Foundation—Tax-exempt organization which makes grants from corpus and income.

Gift—Dispensation of cash, stock, or property generally from individual.

Gift table—Chart of suggested giving levels used in campaigns.

Gifts and records—Department within the development office that records all giving.

Goal—The target set in fund-raising campaigns.

Grant—A sum of money given by a foundation or corporation, frequently for a special project.

Grantsmanship—Techniques used in pursuing grants.

Kickoff—Formal beginning of capital campaign.

Lead trust—A trust which gives its income to charity and retains its principal for a donor or donor's heirs.

Leadership—Board members or others providing fund-raising support to institutions.

Leadership gift—A contribution—from someone normally affiliated with the organization in a voluntary role—that, by virtue of its size, can motivate and serve as an example to others to contribute generously.

Major gift—One of the largest gifts to an institution.

Memorial opportunity—Similar to naming opportunity, it commemorates donor.

Naming opportunity—Recognition given to donors in form of named facilities, chairs, etc.

Peer principle—Concept that gifts are best raised by peers asking peers.

Percentage giving—Suggested levels of giving, usually indicated in corporate drives based on size of company.

Philanthropy—Entire field of charitable giving totalling $50 billion.

Planned giving—That aspect of the development operation concerned with securing short- and long-term contributions through negotiated tax-related agreements with individual donors.

Plaque—Object commemorating gift and memorializing donor.

Pledge—Commitment in principle that a donor will make a gift.

Pledge period—Time during which gift is to be paid.

Pooled income fund—Institution-managed, mutual-type fund that pays lifetime income to donors, with the principal going to institution upon death of income beneficiary.

Proposal—Prospectus written to solicit funds.

Prospect—Someone thought to be a possibility for major donation.

Resident director—Person hired to manage special funds campaign.

Seed money—Early funds given to launch a new project.

Sequential fund raising—Method of starting with major donors and working down.

Solicitation—The process of asking a donor for money.

Telethon—Mass use of telephones to secure gifts from constituency.